THE COMPOSITIONAL MATRIX

Da Capo Press Music Reprint Series

THE COMPOSITIONAL MATRIX

By Allen Forte

DA CAPO PRESS · NEW YORK · 1974

Library of Congress Cataloging in Publication Data

Forte, Allen.
  Compositional matrix.

  (Da Capo Press music reprint series)
  Analytic studies of the Beethoven sketches.
  Reprint of the ed. published by the Music Teachers National Association,
Baldwin, N.Y.
  1. Beethoven, Ludwig van, 1770-1827. 2. Composition (Music) I. Title.
[ML410.B4F6434   1974]   780′.92′4   73-4337
ISBN 0-306-70577-X

THE COMPOSITIONAL MATRIX

To

MILTON BABBITT

THE COMPOSITIONAL

ALLEN
FORTE

MONOGRAPHS

IN

THEORY AND

COMPOSITION

1

MUSIC TEACHERS NATIONAL ASSOCIATION

INTRODUCTION

In the various efforts which we have made to extend our knowledge of musical structure we have all too often shown a curious disregard for the compositional sketches, drafts, and revisions of the major tonal composers. Yet, now that the attention of serious musicians once again is being directed to the Beethoven sketches,[1] the largest body of such materials belonging to a single composer, there is reason to hope that we have gone beyond the stage where these invaluable records were regarded only as memorabilia, to be piously exhibited during centennials, and perhaps have progressed even beyond the stage where they were valued only as bases for musicological inventories; surely it is time that we begin to look upon them as indicators, incomplete though they may be, of the composer's musical concepts and techniques.

Interpretation is therefore the main task. It begins with the transcription of the sketches into legible notation, continues by determining their chronology, and concludes with an explanation of the relationships which are revealed under careful examination. From this a great deal can be learned about concepts and compositional technique— provided there is an initial correspondence between them and the analytic-interpretive means. Such a correspondence is established when the analytic procedures derive from certain basic concepts of structure which they share with general compositional procedures known *a priori*. In the present study two traditional practices which embody concepts shared by the analysis and composition of tonal (triadic) music provide the necessary bases for interpretation. I shall explain these further on, after I have introduced the materials with which we are to be concerned.

BEETHOVEN'S SKETCHES

IN COMPARISON

WITH

THOSE OF OTHER COMPOSERS

Certain distinctive characteristics of Beethoven's sketches become evident when they are compared with those of his contemporaries and successors. First, in sheer number they are impressive. Joseph Schmidt-Görg[1] estimates that over five thousand pages are extant, whereas we have only a handful of sketches from the other major tonal composers. Second, Beethoven's sketches are highly diversified. They include motives and figurations hurriedly notated, melodic outlines of entire sections, detailed and often numerous variants of short passages, and rough drafts of entire movements. In comparison, the sketches which Haydn set down in his notebooks during the years 1793–1796 (for *Die Schöpfung*, *Symphonies 99* and *100*, and smaller instrumental works) are largely drafts of longer passages. Even the more fragmentary sketches, such as those for the last movement of *Symphony 99*,[2] do not bear the signs of intensive revision and development which characterize Beethoven's sketches.

From the accounts of Hertzmann,[3] Newman,[4,5] and Epstein[6] one can conclude that Mozart's sketches, as well as those incomplete works which resemble sketches, are also in the form of more extended drafts. And Deutsch's commentaries[7] indicate that the Schubert sketches are of two types: (1) beginnings of works (like the Mozart fragments) or (2) piano scores for incomplete orchestral works. Preliminary studies like Beethoven's are not characteristic of these three composers.

Beethoven's successors adopted various procedures. Mendelssohn preferred to draft long sections and then revise, his revisions resembling Beethoven's in many respects: painstaking alterations of rhythm and melodic shape which ultimately bring about a marked transformation of the original passage.[8] Schumann's sketches for the *Album for the Young* are more or less complete drafts of the final versions,[9] while his sketches for the *Symphony in Bb major* take the form of an incompletely worked out piano score, many measures of which either contain only the main melodic line or are entirely blank. Two sketches by Chopin, for the *Waltz in Db* and for the *Berceuse*, testify, as do the changes in his manuscripts, to the care which he lavished upon minutiae.[10] This is particularly evident in the *Berceuse* sketch, where each phrase above the repeated bass figure was subjected to intense scrutiny. But again we find no preliminary studies. Chopin's sketches are much more like final drafts; the corrections have been completed and the next step presumably was the fair copy. As for Brahms, Orel[11] has described the three sketchbooks in the Vienna Stadtbibliothek, one of which contains twelve pages of studies for the *Haydn-Variations*. Although Brahms deals with certain of the rhythmic and melodic details in these sketches, he, like Schumann, tends rather to outline large sections, notating clearly the essential features of each variation. Relevant to the present study is Orel's observation that the sketch of the finale exhibits a clear distinction between the basic voice-leading, notated in ink, and the details, notated in pencil, presumably later. Orel also remarks: "These measures demonstrate that the elements essential to the final version are present even in the first draft."[12] Certainly the same cannot be said of Beethoven's sketches, for in many instances one can hardly recognize the final version from the initial sketches.

This brief introduction is not intended to suggest that the sketches of major composers other than Beethoven are unworthy of study. On the contrary, thorough going studies of these materials are urgently needed. However, Beethoven's diversified sketches afford an opportunity to obtain a more extensive look at compositional procedure and also permit bolder speculations regarding the structural conditions which determined his choices.

THE

STUDY

OF

BEETHOVEN'S SKETCHES

A brief account of the serious study of Beethoven's sketches may serve to provide perspective for the present effort. The role of pioneer belongs to Gustav Nottebohm (1817–1882), who transcribed passages from a number of sketchbooks and commented upon them, mainly specifying dates of composition and indicating close chronological connections between works which ostensibly belong to different periods. In his books[13, 14, 15] (recommended for publication by Brahms) he also described certain general features of Beethoven's method of composing, for example that Beethoven often returned to themes which he had jotted down years earlier in his notebooks. Thus, the opening theme of Op. 111 is found in somewhat different form in a notebook which dates from the year 1801.

However, from the viewpoint of the present-day student Nottebohm's achievement requires qualification. He is often apt to regard Nottebohm's commentaries as little more than descriptions of obvious characteristics. And Schmidt-Görg has pointed out candidly that Nottebohm extracted only those sketches which were most legible, and that even then he made a number of gross errors in transcription.

Heinrich Schenker was first to employ the sketches toward the solution of structural problems and to begin to interpret them adequately. This is particularly evident in his explanatory edition of Beethoven's Op. 111[16] where he often refers to sketches of passages in both movements in order to clarify problems of continuity and to explain corrections in the two autographs. However, Schenker did not attempt to specify compositional determinants, probably because of the limitations of that "practical" edition, nor did he make extensive use of the sketches in his later writings. Thus, even his comments on the three extant sketch-pages for the last movement of Op. 27/2 are very reserved in comparison with those which he makes on the autograph revisions.[17]

It should be stressed here that the difficulties of working with the sketches are numerous. The deciphering of the notes alone requires a quasi-cryptographic method, and placing the sketches in correct chronological order entails further difficulties. As nearly as I can determine, it was Beethoven's habit to sketch a particular passage, leave space on the page for additional sketches of the same passage and then move to another position on the page or to another page to sketch a different passage. Often he returned to continue the first sketches, or if not, the space was later used for another idea. When we consider that he customarily worked on more than one composition during the same period, with the result that sketches for different compositions are interlarded in the same sketchbook, and that more than one sketchbook was used for a single work[18, 19] we come to appreciate more fully the problems involved in serious study of the sketches.

A major advance in the field of Beethoven studies was taken in 1927 with the publication of the first completely transcribed sketchbook, the *Landsberg Sketchbook*, which dates from the years 1799–1801.[20] Unfortunately, this advance was not sustained by further efforts until 1952, and even at present the prospect of a *Gesamtausgabe* of the Beethoven sketches remains remote.

Paul Mies has written extensivley about the Beethoven sketches[21] and about sketches and other documents in general.[22] In his work on the Beethoven sketches he categorized specific structural events, for example, "upbeat" and "melodic apex", identifying them as "style determinants", then demonstrated how the transformations evident in the sketches are in accord with them. While this is not the place for a critical review I would like to express the opinion that the categories of events established by Mies are derived from a greatly oversimplified concept of structure. As one important consequence of this he completely neglects voice-leading over the longer span as it affects the shaping of detail. And both he and Engelsmann[23] disregard the influence upon composition of the traditional practices of figured bass and diminution.

The history of serious published studies of the Beethoven sketches ends with a brief but interesting account by Oswald Jonas.[24]

THE SKETCHES FOR OPUS 109

Characteristically, the sketches for Op. 109 are distributed amongst four sketchbooks. In the Deutsche Staatsbibliothek, Berlin, is a sketchbook, designated "Grasnick 20b", which contains five pages of sketches for the first movement.[25] Additional sketches for the first movement are found near the end of a sketchbook which has been published by the Beethovenhaus, Bonn (No. 107 in the Beethovenhaus Catalog). All the extant sketches for the second movement and most of the sketches for the third movement are contained in a sketchbook, "Artaria 195", now in the Universitätsbibliothek, Tübingen. Finally, drafts of Variations 2 and 3 are to be found in a sketchbook which belongs to the Gesellschaft der Musikfreunde, Vienna.

INTERPRETING THE SKETCHES

In the following, which constitutes the central part of this study, I have undertaken to interpret certain of the sketches* with reference to the final version of the appropriate movement. Accordingly, I shall begin by presenting an analysis of the first movement, section by section, using an analytic synopsis in order to achieve an efficient over-view.[26] I will then present sketches of selected passages in what I assume to be correct chronological order with respect to each other and to the finished work. In each illustration the sketches are aligned vertically, measure for measure wherever possible, so that comparisons can be made the more easily.**

Thus the analysis of the final version and the commentary upon the sketches are intended to fulfill the primary purpose of the study: to define certain significant aspects of Beethoven's compositional technique with reference to a single complete work. In addition to the sketches I shall consider some of the interesting revisions which were

---

* Since reproduction of all the Op. 109 sketches is not feasible here I have selected those which in my opinion are most interesting and pertinent. However, no sketches have been omitted which have a significant bearing upon the evolution of the composition.

** The reader is referred to Appendix I for an explanation of certain minor changes which render the notation of the sketches more intelligible. Appendix II gives the location of each sketch quoted.

made in the autograph.[27] These are often revealing, since, like the sketches, they reflect forces which are operative in the entire work.

Before proceeding to examine the Op. 109 in detail I would like to review briefly two traditional bases of Beethoven's technique, which, as I stated at the outset, will also serve as foundation for the analysis and interpretation of the sketches.

TRADITIONAL BASES

OF

BEETHOVEN'S

COMPOSITIONAL TECHNIQUE

Any technical study of Beethoven's works must recognize that his compositional technique cannot be understood apart from certain concepts of musical structure which reached a definitive stage of development about a century before the composing of Op. 109. Many of these concepts are expressed within the practice of thorough bass. Contrary to a widespread notion, thorough bass is far more than a kind of musical shorthand; rather, it should be regarded as a codification of principles which govern the interaction of moving lines within a tonal context.[28] This means that unless certain of the more basic concepts implicit in thorough bass are grasped it is almost impossible to cope with the complex structure of composed tonal music at any other than the surface level. Therefore in preparation for the analysis which is to follow I draw illustrations of two of these concepts from Heinichen's famous tome.[29]

EXAMPLE

1a

1b

When, in order to explain the structure of the model recitative passage shown in Example 1a, Heinichen presents the "fundamental-Noten" shown in Example 1b, he assumes that the reader knows that voices may be implied by the bass which are not necessarily present continuously. Thus, although the upper voice D does not occur in m. 4 of the model recitative (Example 1a) it is given in Heinichen's explanatory representation (Example 1b) as the main note in that measure, and is even tied over from the preceding measure.

Associated with this concept of implied retention in the upper voice is the concept of nonconsecutive connection between notes in a melodic line. This is illustrated by Example 2.

2

Here Heinichen presents a "Variation" of a fourth and explains that tones can be interpolated between a dissonance and its resolution without affecting their relatedness. Observe that the second fourth is resolved on a single sixteenth note which follows the main beat, demonstrating that the main voice-leading of a passage can be carried forward by a note of relatively short duration and that the progression remains unaltered by the displacement of one of the voices from its normal metrical position. Similar displacements often occur as the result of diminution, the second traditional practice which exerted a fundamental influence upon triadic compositional techniques.

DIMINUTION

The practice of diminution in the pre-tonal period is elaborately expounded in the Italian instructional treatises of the 16th century. We can obtain a perspective on Beethoven's refined tonally-controlled technique by considering an example of early diminution drawn from one of these, Conforto's small handbook of 1593.[30]

3

In addition to the four shown in Example 3, the author provides twenty-seven different diminutions for the same ascending skip of a fifth.

During the 18th and 19th centuries the practice of diminution is most clearly evident in variation forms.[31] However, it underlies nonvariational compositions as well and is central to improvisation[32] which, as we know, played a major role in Beethoven's musical life. Although it subsequently disappeared from the musical curriculum, diminution was still taught in the later 18th century. Kirnberger,[33] for example, devotes a great deal of attention to it. Near the beginning of his discussion, entitled "Embellished or Varied Counterpoint," he presents the following brief passage:

EXAMPLE

4

He then carefully explains:

Here the bass has an unembellished melody, each note of which constitutes a step. In the upper voice each step consists of four notes, the first of which represents in every case the main note, while the following three are small motions which serve to embellish it.

As part of Beethoven's compositional technique, the traditional practice of diminution achieves great precision. Changes in diminution, whether in the sketches or in the autograph, invariably point to some problem in adjusting detail to the requirements of a longer span. And just as diminutional detail cannot be considered apart from rhythm, so longer melodic segments cannot be separated from harmony. This is amply demonstrated in the sketches for Op. 109, where the melodic line alone often has sufficient identity to imply a specific harmonic context.

ANALYSIS

OF

THE

FIRST

MOVEMENT

In order to survey the most essential and characteristic features of the entire movement as efficiently as possible I have constructed an analytic synopsis (Example 5). In accord with the concepts of figured bass and diminution, this designates the formal divisions, shows the main voice-leading, and interprets major structural events. I emphasize that the synopsis is not intended to represent 'all' the events in the composition; its purpose is to represent only the main, or controlling relationships in order to afford a survey of the structure with reference to which the sketches can be interpreted. Therefore, repetitions which do not alter the essential voice-leading have been omitted, and the voice-leading itself has been placed in a single register for greater accessibility. In addition, most of the elaborate diminutions employed by Beethoven are not shown. Diminutional motions between upper voices, for example, are represented only by chords or by the diagonal beam (⟋) which indicates that a line or an arpeggiation connects the two tones involved, but does not effect a resolution of the first into the second.

EXPOSITION, MM. 1–8: FIRST THEME AND TRANSITION TO SECOND THEME

The first four measures (plus the initial upbeat) contain the thematic statement, the first complete projection of the triad. By means of half notes, the stems of which point in opposite directions, the synopsis shows that both the third and the fifth of the triad* are established as stable melodic points in the upper voice. The possibility for interaction of these two notes and for their connection by means of the passing note A (or A♯) is implicit. Indeed, it will become increasingly clear that to a considerable extent the melodic development of the movement resides in the composing-out of relationships which are inherent in the upper third of the triad, where A plays a primal role. The first indication of this is given at the end of m. 8 where I moves to II♯ . This latter harmony, which presumably is to be the dominant of V (shown in parentheses), does not resolve as expected. Instead, its upper voice A♯ descends to A♮ over a diminished seventh chord, which constitutes the beginning of the second theme (*adagio espressivo*). Thus,

---

*Throughout this study the expressions "the triad" and "triadic" refer exclusively to the tonic triad.

EXAMPLE

5

the harmonic-melodic progression has suggested but not completed the connection between triadic third and fifth, and although the deceptive progression restores A♮, the melodic meaning of this note is made very ambiguous by the diminished seventh harmony—intentionally so, for in his initial sketch of the second theme the composer provided it with a harmony which had a far more specific motion-tendency.

EXPOSITION, MM. 9–15: SECOND THEME AND CLOSE

The synopsis shows that the upper voice A connects downward to the inner voice D♯ within the $\frac{6}{4}$, while at the resolution to $\frac{5}{♯}$, A♯ of the inner voice is transferred an octave higher to become the upper voice. On the downbeat of m. 15, V, which was expected after m. 8, is finally reached. It then stands at the head of the development section, with B in the uppermost voice.

The most remarkable event in the second theme concerns A in the upper voice. As indicated above, this note has two possible resolutions: (1) to G♯ which would thus connect the triadic fifth of the thematic statement to the third, or (2) to B via the chromatic passing note A♯. Neither possibility is realized. Instead A is first prolonged by a descent to the inner voice D♯ while the inner voice B♯ (m. 9) moves through B♮ (m. 14) to A♯, which, as already remarked, then resolves to B an octave higher at m. 15. The inner voice B therefore "replaces" the upper voice A and gives the effect of resolving that note upward to B. However, A still remains uncommitted, relating melodically both to the triadic third and the triadic fifth, which, in the absence of a connective, are still maintained as separate points. The detail of the second theme presents many characteristic instances of Beethoven's diminution technique. Perhaps the most striking of these is what might be termed the stabilization of an embellishment which occurs at m. 13 (The reader is referred to the score). The F♯ which occurs there in the soprano, supported by a D♯ triad, is to be equated with G♯ in m. 10 (m. 13 being an embellished repetition of m. 10). The remarkable aspect of this equivalence resides in the fact that, in m. 10, F× occurs as an embellishment to G♯. The subsequent role of F× in m. 13 as a stable or consonant note equivalent to G♯ indicates a developmental trend in tonal music taken as a whole which is exemplified by this particular Beethoven work. The harmonic *raison d'etre* of the D♯ triad which supports F× is to be found in the association of that triad with III, as V of III, and by the pivotal role of III at the beginning of the development where the possibility of connecting triadic third with fifth is realized in a complex way.

Since the development section comprises three distinct parts, each with its own major structural event which is a phase of the total progression, I will deal with each in turn.

DEVELOPMENT SECTION, MM. 15-20: FIRST PART

From mm. 18-21, in the progression from the C♯ minor chord to its dominant, the G♯ major chord, we find two major occurrences: (1) the emergence of G♯ in the upper voice at m. 21 and (2) the motion from C♯ to B♯ in the inner voice at m. 21. Schenker pointed out (in his essay "Vom Organischen der Sonatenform", *Das Meisterwerk in der Musik, Band II*) that the placement of G♯ in the upper register at m. 21 tends to associate it closely with the B in the same register, m. 42, and that the two notes taken together comprise the initial motive of the first theme. He also cites other statements of the motive in the same register at m. 43 and at m. 97.

Observe that inasmuch as the second part of the development begins with III, the G♯ major chord serves both as V of VI and as III♯

DEVELOPMENT SECTION, MM. 22-24: SECOND PART

This brief passage returns G♯ to a register two octaves lower than that in which it occurs in m. 21. The change of register is in preparation for the long ascent which achieves the definitive melodic connection G♯–A♯–B in the following and main part of the development section.

DEVELOPMENT SECTION, MM. 25-42: THIRD PART

Here the synopsis shows how the connection from triadic third to fifth is finally completed. This ascending line is supported by the succession II–V–I within the applied dominant to V (II♯). Not shown in the synopsis are the successively higher registers of the A# and B. Indeed, B at m. 42 occurs two octaves higher than shown here. Thus, in the actual work, the composing-out of the space between the successively higher octaves constitutes a prolongation of the essential voice-leading which Example 5 represents in a single register. The main points in this prolonged ascent are emphasized by changes in dynamics: the score contains a crescendo which extends from G# at m. 26 precisely to A# at m. 33 and another crescendo which begins when B over V is reached in m. 42. Change in figuration also plays an important role: the octaves in the left hand reverse direction when A# is reached at m. 33.

Thus the upper voice of the entire development section may be summarized conveniently in terms of the realization of the melodic connection from G# to B which was prepared during the exposition. The triadic third and fifth are also main notes in the bass progression which supports this upper voice motion.

REPRISE, MM. 48–57: FIRST THEME

In order to facilitate comparison the synopsis of the reprise has been placed below that of the exposition. Because of the ascent from G# to B in the culminative third part of the development section the latter note assumes the main melodic role at the beginning of the reprise. At m. 54, B is heard over V, and immediately there follows a short passage within which B connects downward to G# in the inner voice (bracketed) while D# is superimposed.

REPRISE, MM. 58–65: SECOND THEME

Here, as in the exposition, the second theme begins with a deceptive progression to a diminished seventh chord. But since the voice-leading situation here is completely different in relation to the musical continuum the subsequent events in this section duplicate only superficially those of the second theme in the exposition. A brief account of the three main melodic notes in this section follows.

First, by means of the applied dominant motion in the bass (V of

♮ VI), the upper voice D♮ is made to resolve definitively to C. To amplify, the conditions necessary for the retention of D♮ are negated by the V⁷–I resolution here in the shorter span. The reason for this is not obscure: the composer did not want to suggest closure at this point by a motion from leading-tone to tonic in the upper voice. Thus in order to prevent D♮ from implying a further motion to D♯, in accord with its analogue, A, in the exposition, it (D♮) had to be resolved to B♯ (C) with an appropriate harmony. Had the measures under discussion (mm. 61–62) followed the model of the exposition exactly (mm. 12–13) the following succession would have resulted:

EXAMPLE

6

The G♯ major harmony is obviously unsatisfactory: D♯ is not only present but it also resolves to E as indicated.

B, the second important melodic element in this section, emerges in the uppermost voice on the downbeat of m. 63, then divides after the manner of a unison, generating a line which descends through G♯ to E, at the same time retaining itself until it moves to C♯ at the beginning of the close (m. 65).

G♯ remains in the inner voice until the very end of the section. It is represented by G♮ in the ♮VI (m. 61), moves back through G♯ (bass) to A where it merges with the descending upper voice. At m. 65, following a diminutional motion to E, it is presented over I in the upper register, the same register in which it occurred at m. 21.

The unusual chromaticism of this section is somewhat clarified by the reference to the second theme which occurs in the final variation of the last movement (m. 16–24). There, within an expanded $^6_4$, G♯ occupies a more prominent melodic position than does B, and A is presented more emphatically as an upper auxiliary note than as a passing note. (See Example 36b.)

CLOSE, MM. 65–85

In order to show the final and very elaborate composing-out of the thematic upper third of the triad, the synopsis of this section includes more detail than that of the preceding sections. Both third and fifth are first prolonged by means of diminutional prefixes which are designated by slurs in the synopsis. After the VI in m. 78 parentheses indicate that diminutions which do not affect the voice-leading have been omitted. The brackets enclosing II are intended to indicate its special importance in carrying the motion forward to V. As we shall see in the sketches, Beethoven took great pains to arrange the voices here with regard to spacing and direct connection so that the implicit motion from G# through A# to B is suppressed, and, correspondingly, so that the resolution of A# to G# over II#–V is suggested but not realized.

In the melodic detail of the close we find the descending fourth, or tetrachord, and its counterpart, the ascending tetrachord, serving as prefixes to the main triadic tones. This motion has an interesting history. It first occurs in the opening measures of the movement, where the octave line which prolongs G# is divided into two tetrachords:

EXAMPLE

7

It also plays an important part in the exchange-of-voices technique in mm. 21–22 of the development section, is allied with the descent from B–G# at m. 54 ff., and has many other ramifications. Observe that the descending tetrachord which begins on C# and the ascending tetrachord which begins on F# are complementary with respect to the upper third of the triad: the first moves to the triadic third, the second moves to the fifth. If arranged so as to unfold simultaneously instead of successively we see the pivotal position occupied by A:

8

The ascending diminished tetrachord beginning on F× is a prominent melodic element in the development section, both in the detail and in the longer span (see Example 5, m. 25 ff.). In the development section and elsewhere the tetrachord comprises a second (auxiliary note) prefixed to a third. Its derivation from the main thematic interval, the upper third of the triad, is thus evident. Further, this adjustment of the diminished tetrachord to the triadic interval foreshadows the more highly developed role of the tetrachord in the second movement.

At m. 75 the upper voice seems to be ascending a fourth to B as before; however, A♮ changes from passing to auxiliary note and resolves to G♯ over C♯ in the bass (VI). This motion also serves as a final reference to the 'deceptive cadence' which characterizes the second theme.

Observe the exchange-of-voices at m. 75 in Example 5. The entire close exemplifies Beethoven's refined use of this technique, a less obvious instance of which is illustrated by Example 9.

9

At m. 54 the parallel tenths shown in Example 9 occur for the first time. At m. 63 we find the exchange, in complete form, carried by bass and alto (See Example 5). At m. 66 the tenths succession occurs again between soprano and bass. And at m. 81 we find an incomplete exchange, this time carried by inner voice and soprano. The lacuna helps to explain Beethoven's remarkable treatment of A♮ at m. 85; because the exchange, once begun, tends strongly to complete itself, this note had to be introduced, and once present, its unique position as auxiliary-passing note relating to both B and G♯ had to be accounted for satisfactorily. Further on we shall consider an interesting autograph revision which corroborates the explanation just given.

CODA, MM. 86-98

The coda first presents the main melodic motions in succession. Included are the chromatic and diatonic upper auxiliary notes of B, C♮ and C♯, in mm. 90-91 (cf. second theme, reprise), the latter note strongly implying the descending tetrachord which leads to G♯. Beginning at m. 92 the upper voice carries both the third and the fifth, presenting them in successively higher octaves so that just after the end of the crescendo (upbeat of m. 97) we hear only the third, $\frac{B}{G\#}$, in two different registers. Observe that the final B is in the same octave as B at the climax of the development section, mm. 42-48 (see p. 22).

SKETCHES

FOR

THE FIRST MOVEMENT

EXAMPLE 10, A SKETCH FOR THE FIRST THEME

In almost every respect this ink sketch matches the final version. However, closer examination reveals an interesting discrepancy in the voice-leading: the descending octave line from G♯ to G♯ does not occur; instead, the line proceeds only as far as B (in the third complete measure). This suggests that only after working out the entire movement in some detail did Beethoven realize the significance of the descending tetrachord in relation to the thematic third.

In this sketch he seems to give all his attention to the ascending third in the upper voice, E–F♯–G. Observe the cancellation on the second quarter note in m. 3, which indicates that the ascending third was not expressed adequately with F♯ falling after the beat, as it does in the cancelled figure.

The cancellation of the bar line in this sketch shows that Beethoven had difficulty with the unusual upbeat which appears to contradict the bar line accent. It would seem that he had not yet grasped the relationship between the metric plan and the unfolding tetrachords.

Examples 10b–e clarify his anomalous treatment of meter in this instance and suggest a general relationship between rhythm (of which meter is an aspect) and melody.

If the beginning of the theme is rebarred as illustrated by Example 10b, we hear F♯, the second quarter note in the soprano, as an unaccented passing tone. In consequence, G♯ is still understood over D♯, the fourth quarter note, as shown by Example 10c.

Further, Example 10c shows that in accord with voice-leading implications this accentual scheme emphasizes the connection from triadic third to fifth at the end of the phrase.

But by accenting the upbeat, (Example 10d) Beethoven achieves a motion in the upper voice, which centers upon the third (even at the expense of implying parallel fifths).

EXAMPLE

It appears therefore that metric accent is in the service of the unfolding melodic interval. This notion can be extended to the particular way in which intervals are articulated over the longer span. In the development section of the first movement, for example, the measure grouping is determined by the requirement that each phase of the succession $\begin{smallmatrix} 3 & 4\# & 5 & 5 & 3 \\ \text{III} & \text{II}\# & \text{V} & \text{I} & \text{I} \end{smallmatrix}$ be completed on a downbeat (in accord with the definitional value which in the thematic statement has been assigned to the downbeat) and partly by the diminutional figure spanning an ascending third, which establishes its own rhythmic-metric conditions in the shorter span.

EXAMPLE 11, TWO SKETCHES FOR THE SECOND THEME

EXAMPLE

11a

Example 11a, a pencil sketch, shows clearly that the second theme derives from the melodic motive A–G#, which first occurs in the inner voice at the end of the first phrase (m. 3).

This sketch implies the 3/4 meter of the final version. However, in the final version Beethoven (typically) preferred to use smaller note values in order to represent the adagio tempo.

The implied initial harmony, V^7, substantiates the analysis, which regarded the diminished seventh harmony of the final version as a displacement of V.

In Example 11a, as in the final version, we find an embellished repetition of the theme. The diminutions contained in this repetition closely resemble those of the thematic statement (mm. 9–11) of the final version (with respect to pitch), thus illustrating an important role played by melodic diminution in shaping the composition: what was an embellishment of a statement becomes the initial statement itself (cf. explanation of m. 13, p. 21).

11b

Example 11b, which postdates Example 11a, includes the introductory passage to the second theme. This consists of an arpeggiated tonic triad followed by two notes which imply the secondary dominant harmony to V. Observe that Beethoven has sketched here a very direct, concise transition which carries out the harmonic task, tonicization of the dominant, as well as the melodic task, change of register. The final version extends this passage, first by introducing the dominant earlier (m. 6), then by prolonging it until the change of register is completed.

EXAMPLE 12, AN INCOMPLETE SKETCH FOR A PASSAGE IN THE DEVELOPMENT SECTION

In this sketch (Example 12a) we have the first indication of the long ascent to B in the extreme upper register at m. 42. That B is also intended to be the terminal note in the shorter span of this introductory passage is indicated by the final notes in the sketch, G# and A. However, the sketch represents an unsatisfactory solution, as can be seen by comparing it with the final version and with the development section as a whole. With the aid of the bass line of the final version, Example 12b realizes the voice-leading implications of the sketch. The problem lies in the continuation of the motion G# –A. In the implied context this motion either would have returned, not to B, but instead to G# over E in the bass (1) or to G# over C# (2). And although the voice-leading shown at (3) achieves the succession G#–A#–B in the upper voice the inner voice motion is unsatisfactory. Because of the impending parallel fifths with the bass, B cannot descend through A# to G#, but must ascent to D#. From this point the exchange-of-voices between B and G# which is essential to the final version, cannot be obtained (see Example 12c, mm. 21–22). By comparing the synop-

EXAMPLE

12a

12b

12c

12d

12e

12f

sis of the final version (Example 12d) with the sketch and the realization of its implications (Example 12b) we see how Beethoven solved the problem. The voice-leading of Example 12d has been expanded by sequential lower auxiliary notes so that the motion from G# to A does not occur in the inner voice as at Example 12b; instead, the upper voice reaches G# precisely over III#. The exchange-of-voices then occurs entirely within the mediant harmony, pointing up the unique position of that harmony in the total composition.

Example 12e represents the second beat of m. 19 as Beethoven first notated it in the manuscript, while Example 12f shows the revised version.

The revision was made in consideration of the following conditions. The upper voice spans a fifth from C# to G#. In the final version this interval is traversed in two symmetrical motions of thirds (observe brackets in Example 12d). However, if F# is substituted for D# on the fifth quarter note, as in Beethoven's original notation, the symmetry is broken, not only because the sequential pattern of lower auxiliary note prefixes would thereupon be interrupted, but also because F# tends to associate itself with the following F# on the same beat in m. 20, with the result that the E on the downbeat of m. 20 might be heard as a lower auxiliary note between the two F#'s. Its function as the point of departure for the second ascending third would thus be adversely affected.

EXAMPLE 13, A SERIES OF SKETCHES FOR THE DEVELOPMENT SECTION

This sketch-series is accompanied by a rhythmically simplified representation of the final version of the passage (Example 13d) and a synopsis (Example 13e) which shows the essential voice-leading.

The first sketch (Example 13a), evidently Beethoven's first plan for the final part of the development section (mm. 40–42), shows a line rising from F# to a succession of B's. The second sketch (Example 13b) extends by an octave the compass of this ascending motion, and replaces the fourth, F#–B, with the thematic third, G#–B, now expanded to a diminished tetrachord by the adjacent tone, F×. This permits the long span of an ascending third to be traversed by means of motions of ascending thirds—thus, a further integrative factor. After the first B in the upper voice is reached, Beethoven notates the bass. Observe the A♯–A♮ succession, which strongly suggests a resolution to G♯. In the final version he abandoned this in favor of a motion in tenths parallel to the upper voice, a succession which reintroduces the triadic third, G♯, below B, the main tone in the development section. I shall return to this adjustment shortly.

Example 13c is very close to the final version. The arpeggiation from B to B at the end of the passage in Example 13b is now replaced by a continuous stepwise ascent to the final B. Lower auxiliary notes have been introduced in mm. 27 and 29, and a complete auxiliary note serves as a diminution of A♯ mm. 33–34. The final version includes an auxiliary note to F♯ in m. 31, and therefore is one measure longer than the longest sketch.

Observe that the bass line at the end of Example 13c now includes the lower auxiliary note. The reason for this is shown in Example 13e, the synopsis. When the dominant harmony is reached (m. 42) it contains no fifth; the fifth is subsequently given as a passing note in the tetrachord which ascends from D♯. This ascending tetrachord is of considerable importance since it leads to the triadic third at the beginning of the reprise (m. 48). Further, with respect to the two notes which comprise the upper third of the triad, it complements the tetrachord beginning on F× which spans the entire development. These two tetrachords (shown in Example 13f) therefore constitute a direct compositional extension of the complementary relation which was illustrated by the tetrachordal pair in Example 8.

EXAMPLE

EXAMPLE

13a

13b

13c

13d

13e

13f

EXAMPLE 14, A SKETCH FOR THE CLIMAX OF THE DEVELOPMENT SECTION

EXAMPLE

14

This sketch, from Grasnick 20b, is of considerable interest since it indicates that Beethoven originally planned to have the development section culminate on G# supported by III#. We also see here that the reprise was to have begun directly from III#, with no V involved! (This recalls the problematic retransition of the second movement.) From this sketch we can conclude that the plan to compose-out the upper third of the triad in the upper voice during the development section emerged only as the concept of the entire movement crystallized.

EXAMPLE 15, A SKETCH FOR THE SECOND THEME IN THE REPRISE

EXAMPLE

15

An unusual harmony appears in the sketch of the embellished repetition of the thematic statement (corresponds to mm. 61 ff.): The F# major triad below C# in the melody. It would seem that Beethoven rejected this harmony because he decided to use C (B#) in the melody to correspond to F× at the parallel point in the exposition (m. 13). The very fact that he would even consider abandoning the melodic parallelism between the two configurations, in addition to the complete absence of any indication that he ever contemplated using the parallel harmony (G♯ major—see Example 6) demonstrates his concern with the voice-leading problem inherent in this section.

EXAMPLE 16, A SERIES OF SKETCHES FOR THE CLOSE

This series, like the one in Example 13, illustrates the expansion of a voice-leading plan of relatively limited extent. What in the final version is the close, mm. 75–85, is first suggested by the outer voices sketch shown at Example 16a. The soprano carries an upbeat comprising three eighth notes which terminates on G♯, while the bass line moves from V through the chromatic passing tone, B♯, to VI. Subsequently both soprano and bass move from fifth to tonic, a motion which corresponds to the close in mm. 85–86 of the final version. There, however, the upper voice skips from the fifth not to the tonic, but to the third.

In the final version a passage of considerable length is interpolated between VI and V as they occur in the initial sketch (Example 16a). Certain significant aspects of the evolution of the interpolated passage are disclosed by the other sketches in the series. Thus, although Example 16b terminates on G♯ , as does the final version, it is evident that the composer contemplated ending with a direct statement of the auxiliary note figure G♯ –A–G♯ , a relationship which is treated much more sensitively in the final version. Example 16c, the third sketch in the series, makes clear the significance which Beethoven attached to the final statement of the thematic interval G♯ –B. He took care to assure that the upper third of the triad remained "open" at the end of the movement, that is, that the third and the fifth remained unconnected. Accordingly, G♯ is left by skip and B is approached via the suspended C♯ . Beginning at the measure which corresponds to m. 82 of the final version the connection from A in m. 80 to the G♯ in m. 84 is delayed by the skip down to E and the subsequent ascent from E to G♯ . (A voice-leading synopsis of the passage is provided by Example 16g[1].) Judging from the correction in m. 84* Beethoven at first

---

*In mm. 83–84 of Ex. 16c the smaller noteheads represent Beethoven's first, the larger noteheads a later notation.

EXAMPLE

decided not to state the thematic motive G#–B in the final phase of the closing section, but instead to end with the emphasis upon the triadic fifth. This is indicated by the skip from F# to B and by the chords after m. 85 which present the fifth above the triad in three different registers. Of course, in the final version the twelve measure coda stands between m. 85 and the terminal chord.

EXAMPLE

16d[1]

16e[1]

In Example 16d, the fourth sketch in the series, we find the C# in m. 84 restored. Observe that its suspension over the bar line (in imitation of m. 78) is carefully marked by the figures 9–8. This motion is especially meaningful here since it implies the descending tetrachord, C#–G (see Example 8) and thus a final descending connection from triadic fifth to third. However, in this sketch Beethoven still seems undecided regarding the G# in the melody. The bass passing tone A# leads to A♮ on the downbeat of m. 84 (instead of to G# as in the final version) implying that F# is retained in the upper voice as shown in Example 16d[1], which realizes the voice-leading implications of the sketch.

In Example 16e, the fifth sketch, G# finally appears in the upper voice at m. 84. Accordingly, the bass moves to G# on the downbeat, replacing A♮ in the previous sketch. Example 16e also includes the inner voices, and is especially complete when the bass progresses from F# to B, the applied dominant motion. It is apparent that even in the details of voice-leading the composer is concerned about connecting B and G#, for as Example 16e[1] shows, the inner voice motion A#– B—A♮–G strongly suggests a descent from B to G#. Beethoven tries to avoid this implication by spacing the voices widely and by giving the chromatic descent to the tenor. That he considered even this to be unsatisfactory is demonstrated by an ingenious revision in the autograph. First he notated the succession as shown in Example 16f, which is like the sketch, then changed it to read as it does in the final version shown directly below in Example 16g. There A♯ does not move to A♮, but instead A♮ occurs as an accented passing tone in the line just above the bass. This lower voice, A♮, serves as a referent to the connection G♯–B, yet the two points remain unconnected. In this way the very carefully planned succession preserves the ambivalence of A♮ and A♯ in relation to the triadic third and fourth. Those editors who have taken it upon themselves to correct Beethoven's voice-leading in this passage by moving A♯ directly to A♮ in the same voice have destroyed the subtle interaction of the three main melodic elements, B, G♯ and A, which dominate the entire work.

The significance of Á in m. 85 far outweighs its brief duration (cf. Example 1), for it relates not only to the fundamental triadic third and fifth but also to the ascending and descending tetrachords which derive from the linear association of all three elements: third, fifth and the auxiliary-passing note A itself.

Several details in the final version (Example 16g) are now clear. First, the tetrachord in the alto voice which ascends from E♯ to A in mm. 79–80—a reference to the upper voice diminution in the development—here is coordinated with prolongation of A over II^6. This tetrachord is then imitated in mm. 84–85 by the lower voice motion F♯–B explained above. By comparing the synopsis of the entire section (Example 16g^1) with the initial sketch (Example 16a) we can begin to understand how Beethoven combined harmonic and melodic (diminutional) techniques in order to expand the basic voice-leading; for the summary shows that the succession V–VI–V is expanded primarily by the interpolation of II^6 (which also corrects the potential parallelisms) and that within II^6 occurs the melodic descent from C♯ to A in contrary motion with the ascent from F♯ to A. Relevant to this, observe the intricate lamination of the ascending thirds from F♯ to A. These unfold at different rates of speed—similar to a fugal stretto combined with contractions and augmentations of the subject. Lest it defeat its own purpose the synopsis does not include the prolongation of the $\frac{6}{4}$ by the diminutional suffix in the bass, B–G♯ at m. 83 which serves as a connective to F♯ (II)—also omitted—nor does it show the ascending diminutional prefix from E to G♯ in mm. 82-84 in the upper voice.

Finally, this sketch-series tells us a good deal about Beethoven's manipulation of rhythm. Examples 16a and b show an upbeat consisting of three eighth notes. In Example 16c an upbeat quarter note precedes these. Example 16g shows a logical development of this expansion of the upbeat: each of the original eighth notes, which themselves comprise an expanded upbeat, is given the value of a quarter note upbeat. This demonstrates the familiar principle that tonal function, not metric placement or duration, determines the rhythmic property of a given pitch or configuration. To the performer this means, specifically, that the group of three quarter notes must be projected as a single upbeat.

EXAMPLE 17, A SERIES OF SKETCHES FOR THE CODA

Many references have been made above to the multiple meanings of the auxiliary note figure which dominates this final section. The reversal of the figure in the fifth measure of the first sketch (Example 17a) makes even more evident the passing tone implications of the auxiliary note which lies a whole step above the main note, and thus reflects the dual function of A as upper auxiliary to G♯ and, when chromatically raised to A♯ , as the connective between G♯ and B.

The last five measures of the first sketch contain an arpeggiation of the tonic triad which ascends through three octaves to the high B in the same register as the B at the climax of the development section (m. 42) and the beginning of the reprise (m. 48), indicating that the registral association of these points belongs to an early stage in the composing (see p. 23).

Example 17b does not differ significantly from Example 17a, except that here the composer apparently considered a more elaborate figuration of the ascending arpeggio, undoubtedly intending to continue the sixteenth notes throughout the remainder of the passage. This would have associated the coda more obviously with the ascending arpeggio at the end of the second theme (m. 65) in the reprise.

In Example 17c, the third sketch, Beethoven has rejected the embellishment of the arpeggio shown at Example 17b in favor of the incomplete auxiliary note figure.   The only difference between this sketch and the final version is that the latter omits E from the arpeggiation altogether and presents only the thematic notes G# and B—another indication of the composer's increasing awareness of the basic thematic relationship.

Example 17d, the final version (but without the dotted note rhythm), shows by means of brackets the inner voice repetitions of the auxiliary note figure.   In mm. 88–89 the exchange-of-voices which points up these imitations is modified since an exact exchange would cause D# to fall on the downbeat of m. 89; the diminished fifth thus formed between D# and A in the voice immediately above it would resolve A to G# before the downbeat of the next measure and thus negate the repeated two measure augmentation of the auxiliary note motive (mm. 89–90 and 91–92).

EXAMPLE 18, A SKETCH FOR THE FINAL MEASURES

Example 18, like the succession of three chords shown at the end of
Example 16c, relates to the last two measures of the final version. In
this sketch we again see the importance which the composer assigned
to the upper third of the tonic triad. The thirds as well as their inversion, the sixth, in the second measure foreshadow the final version of
the ascending arpeggio at the close of the movement, from which, as
remarked above, the tonic is excluded.

EXAMPLE

18

ANALYSIS

OF

THE

SECOND

MOVEMENT

As is the case with the analysis of the first movement, the following analytic description is not intended to include all the integrative relationships but only to provide a background for the interpretation of the sketches. The analytic synopsis does not, for example, emphasize melodic continuity in the upper voice over the longer span—although this is implicit—nor is the full significance of the detail of the first theme discussed.

EXPOSITION, MM. 1–8: FIRST THEME, FIRST PART

The most important motion within the thematic statement occurs in the bass: the two descending tetrachords (bracketed) which traverse the tonic octave. Coordinated with this we have in the upper voice a statement of the triadic third, G, followed by a prolongational motion which descends to E at the end of the period, and a more attenuated statement of the triadic fifth, B, via its upper auxiliary note C, which is introduced over the II^7 harmony.

EXPOSITION, MM. 9–24: FIRST THEME, SECOND PART

In this consequent phrase, G is reintroduced via its upper auxiliary note A. The resolution of A is remarkably delayed while a number of melodic relationships are incorporated. First, the upper voice ascends to C. C then resolves to B (8) which has been introduced in the voice above the bass via the chromatic passing note, A♯. In this way the triple function of A as ascending passing note, descending passing note, and upper auxiliary note is expressed in a concise passage over a stationary dominant in the bass. The bass note is retained during the repetitions which follow, thus preventing A from resolving definitively to G until m. 24 where the bass moves to the tonic.

In contrast to its occurrence in the initial period the motion C–B in this phrase receives considerable emphasis. However, it should not be regarded as an independent figure, relating only to the triadic fifth (as in the first movement) but rather as a part of the more integral descending tetrachord, C–B–A–G which is implicit here (NB. Example 23, m. 7).

48

EXPOSITION, MM. 25–28: TRANSITION, FIRST PART

As indicated by the synopsis, an arpeggiation of the tonic triad begins in this section. Within the arpeggiation we find two motives from the first theme serving as diminutions: the descending third below G and the auxiliary note figure around B.

EXPOSITION, MM. 29–42: TRANSITION, SECOND PART

Here an important melodic meaning of the transitional figure becomes clear; it provides a strong statement of B for the first time in the movement. Two overlappings occur above the applied dominant seventh harmony, so that just before the second theme begins, D, not B, is carried by the soprano. The upper voice motion E–D–C#–B may be regarded as a tetrachordal prefix.

EXPOSITION, MM. 43–56: SECOND THEME, FIRST AND SECOND PARTS

The synopsis reveals that the upper voice of the second theme unfolds a descending tetrachord, B–F#. Although this tetrachord lies within the control of the dominant harmony its first two notes are carried by seventh chords, while the last two are carried by a C major triad in the first inversion and by an F# major triad (V of V), respectively.

Within this unfolding tetrachord, the soprano note G is prolonged as shown in the synopsis. The succession of parallel seventh chords continues until G is reached in the bass. Instead of proceeding one degree further to an F# the bass then alters direction in the following way. By means of the $\frac{4}{2}$, the downward resolution tendency of the F♮ in the soprano is reversed; it moves instead to G over a ♮II (Neapolitan) harmony which marks the beginning of the second part of the theme. Precisely at this point Beethoven introduces the melodic motive based upon a skip of a fourth (not shown in the synopsis). This, along with the descending tetrachords carried by the upper voice diminutions, clearly expresses the quartal characteristic which was given by the bass at the outset, and which pervades the entire movement.

EXPOSITION, MM. 57–65: CLOSE

Observe the care with which Beethoven avoids the tetrachordal grouping in the descending octave, F#–F#. Specifically, the passing tone E,
which might have been introduced, is omitted. This omission constitutes one of the more enigmatic aspects of the composition (see Example 22a).

DEVELOPMENT, MM. 66–69: FIRST PART

A statement of B within the dominant harmony opens the development. The bass carries the descending tetrachord, B–F#, which in the
subsequent section begins to unfold in the upper voice, as it did in the
second theme. However, here the harmonic context of the tetrachord
differs markedly from that of the second theme.

DEVELOPMENT, MM. 70–96: SECOND PART THROUGH FIFTH PART

Schenker's concept of structural levels is particularly valuable in dis-
closing relationships which underlie the development. Here at the
'foreground' level we find overlapping tetrachords which are complementary (with respect to the octave). However, not all the tones involved in this elaborate pattern are of equal value in relation to the
total span of the development. When we identify the main harmonies
in each section and the upper voice notes which they support it becomes apparent that the controlling melodic pattern, the 'middle-
ground' pattern which spans the entire development section, is the
descending tetrachord, B–F#. In order to clarify the structure of this
section Example 20 provides an analytic reconstruction. This shows,
step by step, the elaborate relationships in the final prolongation of
the tetrachord.

In Example 20a the tetrachord is supported by four different harmonies and three bass notes. In Example 20b the bass takes the leading tone D# which supports a #VII^7. In Example 20c the major third
in the bass between B and D# is partially composed-out by the inser-

tion of C which supports a chord of the sixth. Shown in brackets here are the notes which are to serve as prefix to the latter harmony at the next level. Example 20d, which is very close to the final version, shows how the VI and an applied dominant seventh chord serve to prolong A in the soprano over IV^6. This analytic representation also eliminates change of register so as to show the descending stepwise line, which, departing from G over VI, extends as far as A over $\#VII^7$. The chromatic melodic progression G–G#–A actually is carried not by the upper voice but by the voice above the bass, a technique which belongs to thorough bass and which Beethoven duly noted in his summary thereof.[28]

EXAMPLE

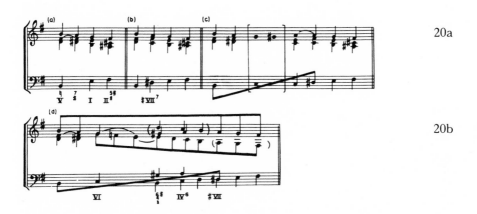

20a

20b

Typical of Beethoven are the ellipsis in mm. 87–88 at the end of part four (see score) and the ambiguous pattern of metric accents brought about by a shift of dissonant and consonant harmonies which support the tetrachord at the beginning of part five (m. 89). This apparent anomaly often distresses performers.

DEVELOPMENT, MM. 97–104: RETRANSITION

The inadequacy of conventional designations for form is particularly evident here, since the actual "retransition" to the tonic begins as early as m. 79 with the pivotal C major triad. But because this section contains one of the most problematic events in the entire composition

I have decided to treat it separately, giving it the conventional label. The problematic event to which I refer is the F# triad which immediately precedes the tonic triad at the beginning of the reprise. Why did Beethoven avoid the dominant harmony at this point? The answer involves the effect of a familiar voice-leading principle upon the tetrachord B–F# which was composed-out during the development. Whether stated simultaneously or successively the interval of a fourth is dissonant and requires resolution to a consonance, normally to either one of two consonant intervals within the triad: the fifth or the third. In the present instance the triadic space defined by the first theme (the upper third) determines the choice of interval of resolution. Thus the fourth, B–F#, expressed linearly by the tetrachord must contract to the third B–G.

EXAMPLE

21a 21b

Example 21a shows that if the final F# is supported by a V^7 this resolution cannot occur since the fourth then necessarily expands to a fifth. In the final version (Example 21b) the melodic requirement of the tetrachord (tonally as well as thematically determined) is at odds with the harmonic requirement, the fifth-relationship expressed by the bass. Beethoven's choice of the F# triad meets the first requirement at the expense of the second.

REPRISE, MM. 105–119: FIRST THEME

The reprise begins with an exact restatement of the first theme. This is followed, not by the second part as in the exposition, but by a repetition of the first part in which the outer voices are inverted.

REPRISE, MM. 120–131: TRANSITION, FIRST PART

The C major triad with which this section begins serves as an excellent example of Beethoven's technique of harmonic association. It is evident that he attached considerable significance to the C major harmony throughout the second movement, for it occurs prominently in the second part of the second theme (m. 52), and in the development section (m. 79). In all three instances it carries the same upper voice note, G, the penultimate note in a descending tetrachord. Thus, the association is more than 'coloristic'; at each occurence the C major harmony designates a specific voice-leading context.

REPRISE, MM. 132–143: TRANSITION, SECOND PART

This phrase, a transposition of mm. 33–42 (but with two measures added, presumably in order to prolong the crescendo) serves to reintroduce the tonic triad supporting G in the soprano.

REPRISE, MM. 144–157: SECOND THEME, FIRST AND SECOND PARTS

This duplicates (a fourth higher) the second theme in the exposition. Considered together, the two tetrachords expressed by the two parallel sections are complementary with respect to the dominant octave (B–B). Thus, whereas the first note of the first tetrachord (exposition) was more important than the terminal note, in terms of the long span, the reverse is true of the second tetrachord (reprise).

REPRISE, MM. 158–167: CLOSE

Here again we have the problematic ellipsis of the passing tone. It seems likely that Beethoven wished to avoid the tetrachordal grouping which would have resulted had the passing tone A been included (Example 22a), since, even though this motion unfolds within the dominant octave, a melodic closure is strongly implied when E is reached.

22a

CODETTA, MM. 168–177

The codetta, where quite different voice-leading conditions obtain, effects the definitive closure, resolving the triadic fifth to the third.

22b

Example 22b shows B in the upper voice prolonged over a I^6 harmony within which the bass descends an octave (observe bracketed tetrachords). Beginning on C in the upper voice of the third measure from the end we have a 'diminutional' tetrachord which supports the more fundamental motion, B–A–G. This is the only reference in the upper voice to the tetrachord. Further, observe that in the codetta as in the close the composer avoids any reference to the tetrachord which descends from B.

Clearly one of the main melodic considerations here is the descent from fifth to third. This may be regarded as a means of preparing the interval—the upper third of the triad—which is to be composed-out in the subsequent movement. Similarly, the bass arpeggiation of the codetta, G–B–E (I^6–V^7–I) prepares for the unfolding thirds in the bass line of the variation theme (see Example 33).

The final bass arpeggiation constitutes a reference to the upper voice of the first theme, a particularly strong reference since we have already heard the upper voice in the lower register near the beginning of the reprise (mm. 112–114).

SKETCHES

FOR

THE SECOND MOVEMENT

Nottebohm made the following statement after having examined
Artaria 195:

The sketches for the second movement . . . are very close to the final version. It can
therefore be assumed that the work for this movement was begun in an earlier
sketchbook.[14]

This statement is misleading in the extreme, for not only do the sketch
fragments represent all stages of composition, but the sketchbook even
contains a long draft, in ink, of the closing and development sections
which differs in almost every important respect from the final version.
One must conclude that Nottebohm's study of the sketchbook was
somewhat less than thorough.

EXAMPLE 23, MM. 1–8: A SKETCH FOR THE FIRST
THEME, FIRST PART

EXAMPLE

23

Perhaps the most remarkable feature of this sketch is the change of
meter from 6/8 to 12/8. Possibly the change has to do with tempo or
perhaps the composer wished to subdivide the bass tetrachord into
two-note groups. Whatever the reasons, the 12/8 meter adversely
affects the integrity of the tetrachord, causing it to sound like a succession of seconds. Possibly the 6/8 meter was restored after the development section had been worked out in some detail, since there the
essential unity of the tetrachord is more apparent.

Observe that the upper voice at m. 7 originally stressed C. Only subsequently did Beethoven subordinate C rhythmically to B, and thus
conceal the relationship between this measure and the codetta, where
C is emphasized in the soprano.

The bass line in this sketch descends the tonic octave without interruption, indicating the extent to which the tetrachordal pattern was predominant even during the early stages of composition. Subsequently, Beethoven inserted the quarter note B in m. 7. The possible reasons for this change are two: (1) he may have felt that the fundamental position V was required to close the period; (2) he may have used the fundamental position V to correct the impending parallel octaves, F#–E, between soprano and bass.

EXAMPLE 24, MM. 9–24: SKETCHES FOR THE FIRST THEME, SECOND PART

In the course of the analysis it was demonstrated that the final version of this passage presented A in relation to both the third and the fifth of the triad. This sketch-series (Example 24) makes clear that Beethoven expended considerable effort to achieve a balance between the two relationships. At (a) we find a descending third, B–G, within which A functions only as a passing tone. The sketch at (b) stresses only the relation between A and B; observe moreover, that the passage terminates on B (asterisk). At (c) we view an attempt to correct the overemphasis upon B; there the passage terminates on G–F# (asterisk).

EXAMPLE

24a

24a¹

24b

24c

It would seem that at least in part the difficulty here concerns the 12/8 meter which Beethoven adopted at one stage (see Example 23). This is particularly evident in Examples 24b and 24c, where the succession of strong and weak measures lends itself to the overlapping two-note, appoggiatura-like figure. One gains some notion of the amount of control which meter can exert upon melodic figures if the final version of this passage is imagined to be entirely in 12/8 meter. Clearly only 6/8 satisfactorily articulates the melody. Other sketches, not shown here, indicate that Beethoven originally intended to use this second part of the first theme again in the reprise. Possibly one reason for not doing so resides in the harmonic similarity between this passage and the second part of the transition in the reprise (mm. 132–143). Were the former to be used in the reprise perhaps it would anticipate the function of the latter and thus create a pointless formal ambiguity.

EXAMPLE 25, MM. 33–42: A SKETCH FOR THE TRANSITION, SECOND PART

This series illustrates the care with which Beethoven developed a melodic line over a harmony which remained unchanged. At (a) we find the octave, F#, in the soprano, at (b) the seventh, E. Presumably because of the similarity between this voice-leading and that of the second part of the first theme (remarked above), Beethoven decided to

EXAMPLE

25a

25b

25c

begin with the fifth as at (c). In the final version he also suppressed by rhythmic means the ascent to the octave (F♯) shown at (c), a motion which, it will be recalled, also occurs in the second part of the first theme.

The problem of meter discussed earlier is still evident in Example 25c, where the first measure of the second theme (bracketed) sounds like an 'upbeat' not a 'downbeat' measure.

EXAMPLE 26, MM. 43–48: A SKETCH-SERIES FOR THE SECOND THEME, FIRST PART

Example 26a, the earliest sketch, begins on the dominant harmony. The analytic sketch immediately below it (Example 26a[1]) reveals that the underlying voice-leading is controlled by the melodic succession B–A–G. This descending line, which continues to F♯(not shown) is represented in the synopsis.

At (b) we see the initial dominant harmony replaced by a diminished seventh chord, and the diatonic melodic succession expanded by means of chromatic passing tones. The diminished seventh harmony suggests the second theme of the first movement. Indeed, the similarity between the two themes becomes particularly convincing when we compare the reprise statement of the second theme of the first movement with the exposition statement of the second theme of the second movement. If Beethoven had retained the diminished seventh harmony for the latter, the harmonies and upper voices of the two would have been identical. A remarkable aspect of this sketch (Example 26b)— one which has to do with Beethoven's concept of form—can be seen in its termination. Clearly the harmonic direction of the passage is changed by the $\frac{4}{2}$ harmony over A♯ in the final measure; this leads to a $\frac{6}{4}$ over B and thence to a *tonic* triad. If one compares this with m. 152ff. of the final version it will become evident that Beethoven has projected his thought towards the parallel section in the reprise.

Even at (c) which has quite a different foreground, the passage moves back to the tonic. Only in this sketch did Beethoven abandon the descending tetrachord in the upper voice.

At (d), F♮ provides the first indication of the role which the Neapolitan harmony is to assume in the second part of the theme.

The sketch at (e) is close to the final version. Observe, however, that Beethoven still retains the initial descending arpeggiation, which serves as a connection to the lower octave.

EXAMPLE

26a

26a¹

26b

26c

26d

26e

EXAMPLE 27, MM. 66–69: THE DEVELOPMENT SECTION, SKETCHES AND A REVISION

Example 27a presents Beethoven's sketch for the opening of the development section. Observe that the progression tends strongly toward a C major triad (C in the bass, G in the soprano) after the last measure, thus forecasting the harmony which is to dominate the third part of the development in the final version.

Example 27b is drawn from the autograph. In order to make the detail of this phrase correspond closely to the initial statement of the first theme Beethoven introduces a rhythmic acceleration in the second measure (m. 67) and thus wins a tenth between the soprano and bass on the downbeat of the third measure. This acceleration permits a more concise statement entirely within the V; it does not permit a phrase extension such as occurs at (a).

The autograph revision shown in Example 27c probably was made in order to permit continuation of the eighth note diminution established in m. 67 (cf. Example 27b). The eighth notes in mm. 68–69 also implement a change of register which is not implicit at (b).

EXAMPLE

EXAMPLE 28, MM. 70–104: A SKETCH FOR THE MAIN
PART OF THE DEVELOPMENT

What is represented in Example 28a as a single, continuous sketch actually occurs in the sketchbook as two separate sketches.   However,
the association of the two is very evident from the handwriting and
from overlapping measures, as well as from the fact that they occur on
the same lines on their respective pages.   (Beethoven often uses this
device in order to mark the location of sketches of the same passage.)
The final version minus what I have designated the retransition (mm.
97–104) extends for twenty-six measures, whereas the sketch shown in
Example 28a is forty-one measures in length.   The structural reasons
for the compression of the final version will become evident as we examine the sketch.

Before comparing the voice-leading of the sketch with that of the final
version, it should be remarked that the transfer of the tetrachord from
bass to soprano (fifth measure) demonstrates conclusively that Beethoven based the foreground upon complementary tetrachords, a relationship which may not be immediately obvious in the final version.
(Tovey and others have referred only to the "canonic" aspect of the
beginning of the section.)

These tetrachords unfold in a highly interesting way. Observe in Example 28b (an analytic representation of Beethoven's sketch) that each
member of a tetrachordal pair differs with respect to internal interval-
succession. The tetrachord which I will designate "antecedent" reads
whole step-whole step-half step, while that which I will call "consequent" reads whole step-half step-whole step (as in a natural minor
scale). Beethoven, when first stating these tetrachords, distinguishes
markedly between them. Whereas the quarter notes in the third measure of each antecedent tetrachord skip a third (as in the theme),
those in the analogous position in each consequent tetrachord skip a
fourth. This skip, which reflects the tonic-dominant relationship,
serves to terminate the octave descent. By manipulating these diminutional skips and/or by stating only one tetrachord of a complementary
pair he can also avoid definition of a particular octave and thus control linear relationships of longer span. For example, by virtue of its
interval succession the tetrachord beginning on G at m. 19 in Example

28a may be considered as the consequent tetrachord in the D octave. Yet, Beethoven does not fully define it as a consequent tetrachord, but supplies it with the skip of a third associated with the antecedent tetrachord. Further, no antecedent tetrachord in the D octave is to be found; the only tetrachords beginning on D are consequent tetrachords in the A octave. Observe also that both tetrachords of the E octave (m. 9ff.) are supplied with antecedent endings, which thus prevent full definition of that octave.

The interaction of the tetrachords is developed carefully in the sketch. This begins with a stretto between antecedent tetrachords, followed at m. 11 by a stretto between antecedent and consequent tetrachords.

Example 28b shows the voice-leading of the sketch in terms of the complementary tetrachordal pairs and thus casts light upon certain problematic passages in the final version. Observe that the consequent tetrachords beginning at m. 17 serve to tonicize VI, and that this major triad is then expressed melodically by major tetrachords which span the octave. (Here of course the distinction between antecedent and consequent is not based upon interval succession.)

The implied bass shown on the lowest staff of Example 28b proceeds by skips of a fourth until C is reached. (This is not to say that each bass point is of equal value; as indicated above, D and G serve to tonicize C, and therefore are subordinate points.) Although the C triad in the final version (m. 79) may well have originated here as a result of the fourths-progression, one must beware of equating the two triads, since the context of the C triad in the final version is far different from that of the sketch. I shall return to this in a moment.

The sketch (Example 28a) ends with the beginning of the reprise. Here we see that the reprise was originally to have begun with the exchange of soprano and bass, which in the final version occurs at m. 112. Further, the reprise was to have been introduced by V^7, an anticipatory entrance of this harmony, coordinated with the close of the consequent tetrachord of the E octave. The sketch shows no trace of the F# triad which holds such a problematic position in the final version. (See p. 68).

With reference to this sketch let us now examine the final version more closely. Example 28c provides an analytic representation. From the outset, where complementary tetrachords unfold in stretto, the final version is far more concise than the sketch. Greater conciseness is further demonstrated in the successive overlapping of antecedent and consequent tetrachords which begin on the same note.

Unlike the sketch, the final version has a bass. Its role is made clear by the two lower staves of Example 28c.

Further, Example 28c discloses the curious position occupied by the A octave. Its antecedent tetrachord begins to unfold at m. 78; the consequent tetrachord, however, does not occur until m. 89. In view of the integrity of the tetrachordal pair and, for the moment, apart from considerations of bass and harmony, the section which extends from m. 83 to m. 88 may be regarded as an interpolation that serves to prolong the antecedent tetrachord. When all harmonic elements are taken into consideration the section can be understood more completely as the fulfillment of the harmonic implications of the antecedent tetrachord (A minor), without at the same time fully defining that tetrachord in terms of the A minor triad. In this way, the composer again solves the problem of bringing the tetrachord over the longer span within the control of the main tonality. A comparison of the two bass lines shown here will amplify this notion. Beethoven does not permit the unfolding tetrachords to dictate the bass and harmony, as in the sketch (Example 28a), but keeps them under the control of the dominant, first by means of the dominant pedal point which suppresses the implied E minor triad, then by means of C which serves as upper auxiliary to the dominant, and finally by completely redefining the consequent tetrachord which begins on D (m. 89) so that its terminal note, A, is carried by the dominant harmony and resolves to G, a motion required by the longer span, as explained above.

Pages 41 and 42 of Artaria 195 contain an even earlier version of the development section than that which is shown in Example 28. Since the degree of correspondence between this and the final version is minimal, extended discussion seems pointless. However, certain features are worthy of mention. The sketch begins with the thematic motives shown by Example 29.

EXAMPLE

29

In addition to these motives, there is prominent one which is derived from the transition (not shown here). Neither the tetrachord nor the descending octave motion appears, but, curiously, an adjacent sketch of a section in E major (Beethoven's key signature) features a line which descends a seventh (Example 30). The relation between this line—with its trivial diminution—and the theme is obscure. Even assuming that Beethoven intended to express an ascending second by means of its inversion, the descending seventh, the ascending second is characteristic of the first movement, not the second. The significance of the E major tonality is similarly problematic.

EXAMPLE

30

SKETCHES FOR THE REPRISE

Pages 48 through 50 of Artaria 195 are given over mainly to a draft of the reprise. This draft repeats certain of the elements of the exposition not found in the final version and even extends some of them, notably the second part of the first theme (Example 31).

Observe the implied Neapolitan harmony in the third measure. In the seventh measure this serves to introduce the dominant which tonicizes the implied C major triad (m. 120 of the final version). The extended Neapolitan relationship—the C major harmony itself served as a Neapolitan in the exposition—is not fully exploited by the composer in the final version.

31

EXAMPLE 32, SKETCHES FOR THE CODETTA

The only feature which Example 32 shares with the final version is the emphasized upper auxiliary note, C. This occurs in the fifth measure and, according to Beethoven's shorthand, is to be repeated four times.

The unresolved seventh in the soprano of the fourth and fifth measures from the end is supplanted in the final version by the two measures which introduce the codetta, mm. 168–169. But here too it is evident that Beethoven planned to end the movement with the third of the tonic triad still active melodically.

The cancellation of E in the second measure of Example 32b suggests the extent to which the composer was aware of the "deceptive" resolution of the soprano F#, in the final version. Subsequent cancellations show that the codetta began as a series of tenths between the outer voices, with the bass carrying the thematic descending octave. This direct succession would have ended in the fifth measure with the third of the triad in the soprano and the tonic in the bass. Beethoven's extension regains the upper auxiliary note, C, which is prominent both in Example 29a and in the final version. In the latter, however, it is more specifically associated with the first theme, as explained above.

EXAMPLE

32a

32b

ANALYSIS

OF

THE

THIRD

MOVEMENT

The analytic synopsis (Example 33) points up the many characteristics which this movement shares with the preceding movements. Here the relationship between triadic third and fifth is composed-out even more directly, more concisely. Observe the connection from G♯ to B which takes place in m. 4. This is not a direct connection, but as shown, G♯ moves to F♯ while A♯ leads to B (the technique which Schenker calls *Uebergreifen*, "overlapping"). The fifth, B, does not constitute the main melodic note in the upper voice, but as in the other movements, only delimits the prolongational upper third of the triad.

EXAMPLE

33

The relationship between the ascending third, G♯–A♯–B and its inversion, the descending third B–A–G♯ (B–A♯–G♯ in m. 12) is expressed in a remarkable way. Thus, in m. 3 the ascending third in the inner voice anticipates the completion of the long ascending third which follows in the upper voice.* The descending third which begins in m. 9 and which effects the return to the main melodic note, G♯, is repeated at m. 12 in the lower voice (tenor) with the chromatic inflection, A♯. An extraordinary interaction of both motions occurs in mm. 5–8. We first hear the descending third, within which the passing tone A is embellished in such a way as to bring about a slight hesitation; this is immediately followed by the direct ascending connection from G♯ to B (cf. m. 4).

---

*In Example 30, thirds of longer span are beamed together, while those of shorter span are bracketed.

At m. 13, the beginning of the last phrase, A serves as upper auxiliary to G#. Subsequently A resolves and in mm. 15 and 16 we have a melodic descent through the lower third of the triad, G#–F#–E. However, in the final measure A is superimposed and reintroduces G# in the upper voice, thus preventing a definitive melodic closure.

The final reference to the melodic relationships which are compressed within the upper third of the tonic triad occurs in mm. 33–35 of the last variation. In those three measures, which comprise a link to the final statement of the theme, A sounds repeatedly against the trilled B, then leads to G# which begins the melody of the variation theme.

The main bass notes and harmonies are directly related to the tonic triad. Particular emphasis is given to III in m. 12, recalling the operation of that harmony in the development section of the first movement. And in the same measure a further association is evident: the retrograde of the melodic ascent which dominates the development of the first movement, G#–A#–B, occurs in miniature in the voice above the bass. Concise references of this kind are not uncommon in Beethoven's late piano works. In the first movement of Op. 78, for example, the succession of three chords in m. 31 marked *forte* summarizes the chord progression of the entire transitional passage, mm. 18–27.

In this movement, as in both previous movements, Beethoven establishes an exchange between the outer voices (indicated by the diagonal lines). The techniques of exchange-of-voices and double counterpoint at the octave are combined in the third variation where the outer voices of the opening of the theme are inverted and supplied with passing note diminutions so as to form double counterpoint at the octave.

At the risk of stating the obvious, I emphasize that Beethoven's use of the techniques of exchange-of-voices and invertible counterpoint as exemplified in Op. 109 derives from the intervallic nature of the thematic statement: the thematic third and the tetrachord to which it gives rise suggest both techniques. Indeed, at one point, mm. 93–100 in the second movement, the techniques become identical.

SKETCHES

FOR

THE THIRD MOVEMENT

In Artaria 195 sketches for the variation theme occur mainly on pp. 36 and 53; many of the pages subsequent to 53 contain sketches for the variations. To my knowledge, sketches for Variation 4 are not extant, although it underwent many changes. Even the· holograph differs markedly from the published score at several points, indicating that Beethoven had afterthoughts as in Variation 3 (see Example 37).

EXAMPLE 34, A SERIES OF SKETCHES FOR THE VARIATION THEME

Example 34 includes all the legible sketches for the variation theme. Some of the salient features of each are described below.

(a) The fifth of the triad is introduced abruptly in the melody at m. 3. The symmetrical measure-grouping of the final version is not yet evident.

(b) Here, as in the final version, the fifth occurs at the end of the phrase. The parallel tenths in the first two measures emphasize the descending thirds in the melody.

(c) The second phrase (m. 5ff.) centers upon the third of the triad, not upon the fifth, as in the final version. In mm. 9–13 Beethoven has sketched in the harmonies below the main melodic notes indicating that even at this stage he was considering variational possibilities implicit in the harmonic succession. The pen strokes in m. 16 of the original suggest that the upper voice F# was notated first, and that A was later superimposed above it.

(d) Here we see the first indication of the descending melodic third, B–A–G#. Observe also that in m. 13 the different stem directions of A and C# reflect their different functions in the melody (A is the main note; C# is diminutional).

(e) In all essential respects the opening phrase is identical with that of the final version. The second phrase, however, effects an octave transfer of B which does not occur in the final version.

EXAMPLE

EXAMPLE

34g

(f) Here we see a further development of the plan for the second phrase shown at (e). The octave transfer has been abandoned; instead an inner voice (D#–E) is superimposed and the terminal note, B, is approached via both its upper auxiliary note, C#, and the leading note. The incomplete bass implies subsequent progression by descending fifth.

(g) This draft, which closely resembles the final version includes a good deal of detail. Observe that the melody of the second phrase (m. 5) was first begun on G#, not B, thus demonstrating the primal function of the third in relation to the fifth. Secondary diminutions were penciled in, presumably later: the arpeggio in m. 5 and the turn in m. 6 (to be read as though the leger lines were below the treble staff). The pivotal role of A as both passing and upper auxiliary note is clearly demonstrated in mm. 10, 13, and 14 where it is notated on the first line above the treble staff in the manner of an organ point. In view of the difficult stretches which would be required to play this A along with the other voices it seems likely that for Beethoven it served only to indicate the central melodic note of the passage.

SKETCHES FOR THE VARIATIONS

Since the sketches for the variations are too numerous to permit extensive quotation and commentary I have selected two for discussion which I believe to be representative of the problems and techniques involved. An interesting autograph revision will provide additional information.

EXAMPLE 35, A SKETCH FOR VARIATION II

This very carefully penned sketch of mm. 9–12 was just as carefully cancelled out by Beethoven. In the final version he decided to omit the appoggiature in the uppermost voice and stress those in the voice below it. The reasons for this may have been several, but unquestionably the most obvious is rhythmic: the upper voice appoggiature cannot be expressed within the rhythmic pattern carried by the repetition of the consequent phrase (mm. 13–16)—and on the basis of the first statement it is expected that they will occur there.

EXAMPLE

35

EXAMPLE 36, A SKETCH FOR VARIATION VI

This is a sketch for mm. 16–24 of the last variation, a passage which bears a strong resemblance to the second theme of the first movement as it occurs in the reprise (m. 58ff). The improvisational nature of both sketch and final version is evident in the frequent anticipations of harmonic change, an intensification of the anticipation which characterizes the second theme. The structural defects of the sketch are illustrated by Example 36b, an analytic representation of the final version.

The beam connects the notes which comprise the main upper voice succession: the thematic descending third followed by the auxiliary

EXAMPLE

36a

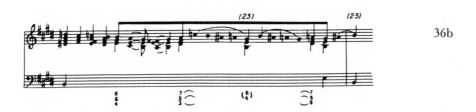

36b

note figure A–G♯–A. In comparison, the diminutions of the sketch obscure these relations. For example, observe the untimely emphasis which the melody of the sketch places upon B at m. 22 and again at m. 24.

AUTOGRAPH REVISIONS

Beethoven made changes at several points in the autograph of the third movement. Perhaps the most interesting of these occurs in mm. 20–25 of the third variation. To assist the verbal explanation Example 37 first presents the corresponding passage in the variation theme (a); the original and final versions, respectively, are then aligned below it (b and c).

EXAMPLE

From a purely pianistic standpoint the register of the first version (Example 37b) is not in accord with the invertible counterpoint that characterizes this variation, for inversion would necessitate an awkward crossing of hands. Therefore in Example 37c, the final version, the lower voice is placed an octave lower.

The one measure (m. 22) which, apart from the difference in register, remains the same in both versions, provides a clue to certain additional determining factors in the revision. Beethoven evidently wanted to continue the preceding stepwise diminutions (which the first version with its arpeggiations does not achieve), yet at the same time desired a distinctive diminutional pattern which would point up the unique and controlling harmony of this phrase (III).

However, the association of diminutional patterns with respect to melody and harmony also affected the revision of this passage. The thematic descending third (bracketed) which occurs in mm. 21 and 23 of the first version is maintained only in m. 21 of the final version since it is impossible to obtain that figure in m. 23 and yet bring the line to the desired goal in m. 24 unless a discontinuous element is introduced, either a skip or a rhythmic accelerando. However, in m. 24 the composer achieves a repetition of the *ascending* third, (see m. 22) which compensates for the discontinuity.

A further structural reason for the revision of m. 21 is shown by the two voice-leading synopses, Examples 37d and 37e. In order to correspond with the theme, the main upper voice note in mm. 21 and 22 must be A (see Example 37a). However, Example 37d shows that the metrically accented C# in m. 21 of the first version leads A, by virtue of its position a third below C# , to B in m. 22. In the diminution of m. 21 of the final version, however, where C# is unaccented (Example 37e) there is no such premature resolution of the A to B; instead, A is retained for two measures. This retention in the upper voice is matched by the retention of A in the bass (the melody of the theme), so that the two A's in the outer voices expand in contrary motion, the upper to B, the lower to G# , a motion which thus emphasizes the position of A as pivotal tone within the triadic third, G#–B, in the variation theme as a whole.

A final aspect of the revision of this passage is to be seen in the last measure, m. 24. On the second beat of the measure (Example 37c) the upper voice E is supplied with a suffix so that the line connects uninterruptedly with the inverted repetition of the passage (in double counterpoint), in accord with the plan of the variation, whereas the first version closes on E, and thus makes no provision for the stepwise continuation of the sixteenth note motion.

On pp. 6–8 of the sketchbook in the collection of the Gesellschaft der Musikfreunde there is a draft of Variation III upon which appear the revisions just discussed. Obviously this draft antedates the autograph revisions, supporting the fact——if it requires support——that for Beethoven the compositional process meant continuous and energetic musical thought.

CONCLUSION

The nature of Beethoven's original musical idea for Op. 109 remains concealed. However, the sketches and autograph revisions suggest that he had in mind a plan for the entire work, a plan which during the compositional process was amplified and refined until all elements had been coordinated to form a cogent totality.

The sketches indicate that Beethoven's concept of the totality extends beyond the individual movements to include all three movements. And analysis discloses a relationship between movements which perhaps is not immediately apparent from study of the sketches: the developmental progression from one movement to the next. This becomes evident, *pars pro toto*, when the bass lines of the thematic statements of each movement are compared.

EXAMPLE

38

In Example 38 we see that the thirds of the variation theme's bass (Example 38c) are implicit in the tetrachords of the second movement (Example 38b, mm. 4 and 8), while both tetrachords and thirds are given by the bass line of the first movement (Example 38a).

The intervallic basis of this extended relationship also enables us to understand more fully the significance of detail, for we see that the first four notes of the composition constitute a microcosm, a concise linear statement of the two intervals which are to control the entire work.

EXAMPLE

39

APPENDIX I

NOTATIONAL CHANGES

In order to make the sketches more intelligible to the modern student certain aspects of Beethoven's handwriting have been conventionalized. This differs from the procedure which the Beethovenhaus has employed in its transcribed sketchbooks. The difference in procedure reflects a difference in purpose, for whereas the Beethovenhaus publications are designed to provide source material in a form as faithful as possible to the original, the present study is intended to interpret source material. Accordingly, notational obscurities in the original sketches have been removed in order to permit the reader to concentrate upon the explanatory text. A brief description of these changes is given below.

DOTS AND STEMS OMITTED BY THE COMPOSER

Beethoven often omitted dots and often failed to provide notes with stems in the sketches. Inasmuch as these notational details are easily understood by the reader no effort has been made to supply them.

UNCLEAR OR ILLEGIBLE PASSAGES

The abbreviation "uncl." (for unclear) designates notes which appear on the sketch page but which are difficult to locate specifically. In such cases I have represented the notes which, judging from the context, I assume to be most reasonable.

The abbreviation "illeg." (for illegible) designates the approximate position of notes which are totally obscured by cancellation marks, blots, foxing, etc. and which therefore are not represented in the quoted sketch.

STEM DIRECTION

The direction of stems has been made to conform to modern practice, since Beethoven's disregard for the middle of the staff as a dividing point which determines stem direction might suggest the presence of other, specific voices to the musician who has been taught to regard the notation of the four-part chorale as a norm.

METER AND TEMPO MARKINGS

All meter signatures and tempo indications are the composer's.

PARENTHESES

Parentheses which enclose notes are of two types, readily distinguishable by their position in the sketch quoted. When they occur in any position other than at the end of a sketch they designate notes which are either unclear or illegible, but which in my judgement are implied by the musical context. If, however, they occur at the end of a fragmentary sketch they designate notes which, in my opinion, would represent a continuation.

CLEFS AND KEY SIGNATURES

Clefs and key signatures have been supplied. Those instances in which Beethoven himself provides a clef are remarked in the text.

ACCIDENTALS

Accidentals other than those provided by Beethoven are enclosed in parentheses.

APPENDIX II

LOCATION OF THE QUOTED SKETCHES

10	GRASNICK 20b:4^V	ARTARIA 195:47	25b
11a	GRASNICK 20b:3^V	ARTARIA 195:43	25c
11b	GRASNICK 20b:4	ARTARIA 195:43	26a
12	BEETHOVENHAUS 107:40	ARTARIA 195:44	26b
13a	BEETHOVENHAUS 107:39	ARTARIA 195:47	26c
13b	BEETHOVENHAUS 107:40	ARTARIA 195:37	26d
13c	BEETHOVENHAUS 107:40	ARTARIA 195:46	26e
14	GRASNICK 20b:3^V, 5	ARTARIA 195:44	27a
15a	GRASNICK 20b:5	ARTARIA 19 :46–7	28
16a	BEETHOVENHAUS 107:39	ARTARIA 195:41	29
16b	GRASNICK 20b:5^V	ARTARIA 195:41	30
16c	BEETHOVENHAUS 107:41	ARTARIA 195:48	31
16d	BEETHOVENHAUS 107:41	ARTARIA 195:45	32a
16e	BEETHOVENHAUS 107:39	ARTARIA 195:50	32b
17a	BEETHOVENHAUS 107:43	ARTARIA 195:53	34a
17b	BEETHOVENHAUS 107:43	ARTARIA 195:53	34b
17c	BEETHOVENHAUS 107:40	ARTARIA 195:36	34c
18	BEETHOVENHAUS 107:41	ARTARIA 195:53	34d
23a	ARTARIA 195:37	ARTARIA 195:36	34e
23b	ARTARIA 195:42	ARTARIA 195:37	34f
24a	ARTARIA 195:37	ARTARIA 195:53	34g
24b	ARTARIA 195:41	GESELLSCHAFT	
24c	ARTARIA 195:42	DER MUSIKFR.:47	35
25a	ARTARIA 195:44	ARTARIA 195:1	36a

NOTES

1   The Beethovenhaus, Bonn, has recently published two complete sketchbooks, the first of a projected series: (a) DREI SKIZZENBÜCHER ZUR MISSA SOLEMNIS I, EIN SKIZZENBUCH AUS DEN JAHREN 1819–1820 (1952) and (b) EIN SKIZZENBUCH ZUR CHORFANTASIE, OP. 80 UND ZU ANDEREN WERKEN (1958).

2   Codex 189, Nationalbibliothek, Vienna.

3   Erich Hertzmann, MOZART'S CREATIVE PROCESS. The Musical Quarterly, April 1957.

4

    Sidney Newman, MOZART'S G MINOR QUINTET AND ITS RELATIONSHIP TO THE G MINOR SYMPHONY. The Music Review, November 1956.

5   Sidney Newman, A MOZART SKETCH-SHEET. The Music Review, February 1957.

6   Peter Epstein, EIN UNBEKANNTER ENTWURF MOZARTS ZUR D-DUR SONATE. Die Musik, September 1926.

Otto Erich Deutsch (comp.), SCHUBERT THEMATIC CATALOGUE, London, J. M. Dent & Sons, 1951.   7

Donald Mintz, MELUSINE: A MENDELSSOHN DRAFT. The Musical Quarterly, October 1957.   8

Oswald Jonas, DAS SKIZZENBUCH ZU ROBERT SCHUMANNS JUGENDALBUM OP. 68. Zeitschrift für Musik, July 1931.   9

TROIS MANUSCRITS DE CHOPIN. Commentés par Alfred Cortot et accompagnés d'une étude historique sur les manuscrits par Édouard Ganche. Paris, Dorbon Aîné, 1932.   10

Alfred Orel, SKIZZEN ZU JOH. BRAHMS HAYDN-VARIATIONEN FÜR ZEWI PIANOFORTE OP. 56b. Zeitschrift für Musikwissenschaft, Vol. 5, 1922–23.   11

"Diese Takte zeigen auch, wie schon im ersten Entwurfe alles Wesentliche der Endfassung im Prinzip Vorhanden ist." Ibid.   12

Gustav Nottebohm, BEETHOVENIANA. Leipzig, 1872.   13

Gustav Nottebohm, ZWEITE BEETHOVENIANA. Leipzig, 1887.   14

Gustav Nottebhom, ZWEI SKIZZENBÜCHER VON BEETHOVEN AUS DEN JAHREN 1801–1803. Edited by Paul Mies. Leipzig, 1924.   15

Henrich Schenker, ERLÄUTERUNGSAUSGABEN DER LETZTEN FÜNF SONATEN VON BEETHOVEN. Vienna, Universal Edition, 1921.   16

17 Henrich Schenker, LUDWIG VAN BEETHOVEN: SONATE OP. 27, NR. 2, FAKSIMILE-REPRODUCTION. Vienna, Universal Edition, 1921.

18 M. Iwanow-Boretzky, EIN MOSKAUER SKIZZENBUCH VON BEETHOVEN. Musikalische Bildung 1–2, 1927. A commentary upon a sketchbook which is reproduced in facsimile in the same issue. The author demonstrates that this sketchbook complements the one used by de Roda (see note 19 for his report.)

19 Cecille de Roda, UN QUADERNO DI AUTOGRAFI DI BEETHOVEN. Torino, 1907.

20 Karl Lothar Mikulicz (ed.), EIN NOTIERUNGSBUCH VON BEETHOVEN AUS DEM BESITZ DER PREUSSISCHEN STAATSBIBLIOTHEK ZU BERLIN. Leipzig, 1927.

21 Paul Mies, DIE BEDEUTUNG DER SKIZZEN BEETHOVENS ZUR ERKENNTNIS SEINES STILS. Leipzig, 1925.

22 Paul Mies, DIE BEDEUTUNG VON SKIZZEN, BRIEFEN, UND ERINNERUNGEN FÜR DIE STILKUNDLICHE FORSCHUNG. Neues Beethoven-Jahrbuch, 1938.

23 Walter Engelsmann, BEETHOVENS KOMPOSITIONSPLÄNE, DARGESTELLT IN DEN SONATEN FÜR KLAVIER UND VIOLINE. Augsburg, 1931.

24 Oswald Jonas, AN UNKNOWN SKETCH BY BEETHOVEN. The Musical Quarterly, April 1940.

25 The contents of this sketchbook are described by Wilhelm Virneisel in his article, ZU BEETHOVENS SKIZZEN UND ENTWÜRFEN, in STUDIEN ZUR MUSIKGESCHICHTE DES RHEINLANDES; FESTSCHRIFT ZUM 80. GEBURTSTAG VON LUDWIG SCHIEDERMAIR. Köln, Arno Volk-Verlag, 1956.

Certain visual devices and analytical procedures used in this study derive from Schenker.　26

The holograph is now in the Library of Congress. The plates for the first edition were engraved from a copy which was made for the publisher after the original, with its many corrections, had caused much delay.　27

Beethoven's studies in thorough bass, species counterpoint, and fugue were first published in 1832 by Seyfried. Subsequently both Thayer and Nottebohm directed strong criticisms at Seyfried for tampering with the original texts and in 1873 Nottebohm published the studies in an accurate form. The composer's respect for these traditional disciplines is reflected in his recommendation that the serious musician carry out an exercise in variation and in counterpoint each day.　28

Johann David Heinichen, DER GENERAL-BASS IN DER COMPOSITION. Dresden, 1728.　29

Giovanni Luca Conforto, BREVE ET FACILE MANIERA D'ESSERCITARSI A FAR PASSAGI. Rome, 1593(?). A facsimile reproduction, edited by Johannes Wolf, was published in 1922.　30

See Hans-Peter Schmitz, DIE KUNST DER VERZIERUNG IM 18.JAHR-HUNDERT. Kassell, Bärenreiter, 1955.　31

See Schenker's essay, DIE KUNST DER IMPROVISATION, in DAS MEISTER-WERK IN DER MUSIK, München, 1925. Also Ernst Ferand's DIE IMPROVI-SATION IN DER MUSIK, Zürich, 1938.　32

Johann Philip Kirnberger, DIE KUNST DES REINEN SATZES IN DER MUSIK. Berlin, 1771.　33

LIST OF UNNUMBERED ILLUSTRATIONS

ACKNOWLEDGEMENTS

Some three years have passed since this study was initiated and planned for publication. During that time a number of persons have been involved, many of whom have assisted directly in overcoming the significant as well as the trivial problems which seem to be inherent in efforts of this kind. To give a complete roster of names would be impossible here. Therefore I express my gratitude specifically only to those who have been directly concerned, but at the same time I wish to convey my appreciation to all the others. Accordingly, my sincere thanks to those in the MTNA who have been involved from the outset: Professor Leigh Gerdine, Professor Charles Garland, Professor Dika Newlin, Professor H. Owen Reed, Professor Albert Seay, and Dr. S. Turner Jones. In addition, I owe a special debt of gratitude to Mr. Ernst Oster for his thoughtful critique of the manuscript and to those who helped me to assemble the source materials upon which the study is based: the late Richard S. Hill, Music Division, Library of Congress, Dr. Köhler of the Deutsche Staatsbibliothek, Berlin, Frau Dr. Hedwig Kraus, Gesellschaft der Musikfreunde, Wien, Professor Joseph Schmidt-Görg, Director of the Beethoven Archiv, Bonn, and Professor Wilhelm Virneisel, Universitätsbibliothek, Tübingen.

BOOK AND COVER DESIGNED BY

SHARLAND

PRINTED BY THE SCIENCE PRESS